21st Century Junior Library

Bullying

by Lucia Raatma

CHERRY LAKE PUBLISHING * ANN ARBOR, MICHIGAN

Published in the United States of America by Cherry Lake Publishing
Ann Arbor, Michigan
www.cherrylakepublishing.com

Content Adviser: David Wangaard, Executive Director, SEE: The School for Ethical Education, Milford, Connecticut

Reading Adviser: Marla Conn, ReadAbility, Inc.

Photo Credits: Cover, ©MANDY GODBEHEAR/Shutterstock, Inc.; pages 4, 8, 10, and 14, ©O Driscoll Imaging/Shutterstock, Inc.; page 6, ©Monkey Business Images/Shutterstock, Inc.; page 12, ©Dora Zett/Shutterstock, Inc.; page 16, ©iStockphoto.com/1MoreCreative; page 18, ©Lisa F. Young/ Shutterstock, Inc.; page 20, ©Catalin Petolea/Shutterstock, Inc.

LIBRARY OF CONGRESS CATALOGING-IN-PUBLICATION DATA
Raatma, Lucia.
 Bullying/by Lucia Raatma.
    pages cm.—(Character education) (21st century junior library)
 Includes bibliographical references and index.
 Audience: K to Grade 3.
 ISBN 978-1-62431-152-9 (lib. bdg.)—ISBN 978-1-62431-218-2 (e-book)—
ISBN 978-1-62431-284-7 (pbk.)
 1. Bullying—Juvenile literature. 2. Aggressiveness in children—Juvenile literature. I. Title.
BF637.B85R327 2014
302.34'3—dc23   2013007031

*Cherry Lake Publishing would like to acknowledge the work of
The Partnership for 21st Century Skills.
Please visit www.p21.org for more information.*

Printed in the United States of America
Corporate Graphics Inc.
July 2013
CLFA13

CONTENTS

Bullies can make kids feel unhappy and uncomfortable.

What Is Bullying?

Nate was walking through the cafeteria at school. Suddenly, Charlie stuck out his foot and tripped him. Nate fell to the ground, and his food scattered everywhere. The kids around him started to laugh.

"What's the matter, Nate? Did you trip over your own feet?" Charlie teased him.

Nate's face turned bright red. He wanted to disappear.

Some bullies make kids feel bad by saying mean things about them.

Bullying is a mean **behavior**. It is a way to make fun of other people. Some bullies pick on kids or say bad things about them. They also keep other kids from feeling like they are part of the group.

Usually, bullying is not a one-time thing. Instead, bullies tease their **victims** over and over.

Think!

Have you ever been bullied? How did it make you feel? Were you scared? Also, have you ever acted like a bully? Think about how your actions can hurt others.

Bullies might make fun of other kids for the clothes they wear or the way they look.

How Bullies Hurt People

Many bullies are mean to people who are different. They call them names. Andrea is a bully. She makes fun of how kids look. Sometimes she jokes about their braces or glasses or wheelchairs. She teases kids about what they wear. Sometimes she even teases people who are from another country or **culture**.

Some bullies use violence to scare other kids.

George often shoves or pushes the people he is teasing. He pulls their hair or knocks them down. Sometimes he even hits other kids. The kids he bullies are sometimes afraid to go to school.

Some bullies spread lies about other kids. They tell mean stories that **embarrass** kids. Bullies can make their victims feel awful.

Bullying can make kids feel like they don't fit in at school.

Bullies might say things like, "You can't play with us." Or they might say, "Don't sit at our table." This is how bullies make kids feel as though they are not liked. Kids who are bullied may feel like they are not good enough to be part of the group. But all kids deserve **respect**.

Look!

Watch the kids on your playground. Are they friendly? Are some of them bullies? See how bullies try to make other kids feel bad.

Bullies often corner their victims in places where adults can't see them.

Bullying can happen just about anywhere. Matt and his friends are bullied on the playground or in neighborhood parks. Sue was picked on in the school bathroom. Bullies can **taunt** kids in the cafeteria or on the bus. Usually, they choose places where adults are watching too many kids at once. Or they find places where there are no adults at all.

Ignoring bullies is often the best way to deal with them.

Ways to Stop Bullying

If you are being bullied, you probably feel terrible. You might want to yell at the bully. Or you may feel like crying. It is best to just walk away from the bully. Pretend that the bullying does not bother you. If the bully does not get a **reaction**, he might leave you alone.

Inviting someone to sit with you at lunch is a great way to help her feel included.

If you see someone being bullied, try to help. Tell the person being bullied to come sit at your table. Offer to be her partner for a school project. With a group of friends, tell the bully to leave the victim alone. Sometimes a bully will be surprised if a group stands up to him.

Create!

Write a play about bullying. Include characters who are bullies and characters who are victims. Have your friends play those roles—and then switch. See how different being the bully feels from being the victim.

Sometimes the only way to deal with a bully is to ask an adult for help.

Sometimes, you will need an adult to help. Martha's friend Thomas was being bullied by a classmate. She told a teacher about it. Often, adults do not know there is a problem until you tell them. They can watch what the bully does. They can find ways to make the bad behavior stop.

Ask Questions!

Talk to a teacher or parent about bullies. Ask questions about why bullies behave like they do. Maybe they are upset and are acting out. Find out if bullies are really sad—not just mean.

GLOSSARY

behavior (bi-HAYV-yuhr) the way someone acts

culture (KUHL-chur) the ideas, customs, and traditions of a group of people

embarrass (em-BA-ruhss) make someone feel awkward or uncomfortable

reaction (ree-AK-shuhn) an action in response to something

respect (ri-SPEKT) a sense of caring for someone else's worth

taunt (TAWNT) to make people upset by teasing them

victims (VIK-tuhmz) people who are mistreated or hurt by something

FIND OUT MORE

BOOKS

Hall, Pamela. *A Bully-Free Playground*. Minneapolis: Magic Wagon, 2013.

Hall, Pamela. *A Bully-Free School*. Minneapolis, MN: Magic Wagon, 2013.

Sornson, Robert, and Maria Dismondy. *The Juice Box Bully: Empowering Kids to Stand Up for Others*. Northville, MI: Ferne Press, 2010.

WEB SITES

Dealing with Bullies
http://kidshealth.org/kid/feeling /emotion/bullies.html
Find out about bullies and how to handle them.

Stop Bullying
www.stopbullying.gov
Learn about bullying and how to prevent it.

INDEX

ABOUT THE AUTHOR

Lucia Raatma has written dozens of books for young readers. They are about famous people, historical events, ways to stay safe, and other topics. She lives in Florida's Tampa Bay area with her husband and their two children.